D0049512

Seeds

by Gail Saunders-Smith

Photo: Blue Lupine Seeds

Content Consultant:
Deborah Brown, Horticulturist
University of Minnesota Extension Service

Pebble Books

an imprint of Capstone Press

1

Pebble Books

Pebble Books are published by Capstone Press
818 North Willow Street, Mankato, Minnesota 56001
http://www.capstone-press.com

Library of Congress Cataloging-in-Publication Data
Saunders-Smith, Gail.
    Seeds/by Gail Saunders-Smith.
        p. cm.
    Includes bibliographical references (p. 23) and index.
    Summary: Simple text and photographs depict types of flower seeds, how they travel, and
what happens when they are planted.
    ISBN 1-56065-771-5
    1. Seeds -- Juvenile literature. 2. Flowers -- Seeds -- Juvenile literature. [1. Seeds. 2. Flowers.] I. Title.
QK661.S37 1998
575.6'8--dc21   98-5048
                                                                        CIP
                                                                         AC

Note to Parents and Teachers

This book describes and illustrates types of seeds, how they travel, and what happens when they are planted. The close picture-text matches support early readers in understanding the text. The text offers subtle challenges with compound and complex sentence structures. This book also introduces early readers to expository and content-specific vocabulary. The expository vocabulary is defined in the Words to Know section. Early readers may need assistance in reading some of these words. Readers also may need assistance in using the Table of Contents, Words to Know, Read More, Internet Sites and Index/Word List sections of the book.

2

Table of Contents

Kinds of Seeds 5

How Seeds Are Planted 9

Note to Parents
 and Teachers 2
Words to Know 22
Read More 23
Internet Sites 23
Index/Word List 24

Seeds

A flower is the part of a plant that makes seeds. Seeds form after the flower blooms. New plants can grow from seeds.

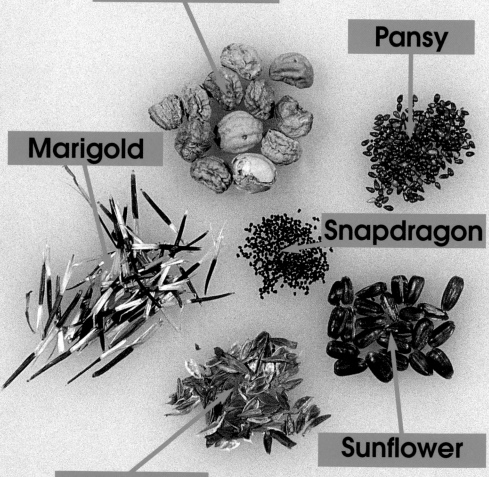

Nasturtium

Pansy

Marigold

Snapdragon

Sunflower

Zinnia

Flower seeds are different sizes, shapes, and colors. Some seeds are long, and some are short. Some seeds are small, and some are big. Each kind of seed grows into a different kind of flower.

People plant flower seeds. They place the flower seeds in holes in the ground. People cover the seeds with soil. Then they water the seeds.

Seeds

New Plants

10

Nature also plants flower seeds. Some seeds fall from the old flower. These seeds go into the soil. New plants grow near the old plants.

Birds eat flower seeds. They scatter some seeds on the ground. They drop some seeds in places far away.

The wind moves seeds. Some seeds have soft hairs. These hairs catch the wind. The seeds float to new places where they can grow.

Seeds need air, water, and warmth to grow. They also need food found in the soil.

A seed takes in water. Then it breaks open. A new plant is inside the seed.

The new plant grows roots.
Roots grow down. The new
plant grows a stem. The stem
grows up through the soil.
The stem grows into a flower.

Words to Know

roots—a part of a plant that grows in the ground; roots take in water and food from the ground and carry them to the rest of the plant

scatter—to drop things in many places

soil—dirt or earth; plants grow in soil

sprout—to begin to grow; the first shoot out of a seed

stem—the long part of a plant that grows above ground; leaves and flowers grow from the stem

Read More

Berger, Melvin. *All about Seeds.* New York: Scholastic, 1992.

Gibbons, Gail. *From Seed to Plant.* New York: Holiday House, 1993.

Hickman, Pamela. *A Seed Grows.* Toronto: Kids Can Press, 1997.

Marzollo, Jean. *I'm a Seed.* New York: Scholastic, 1996.

Internet Sites

4-H Children's Garden
http://commtechlab.msu.edu/sites/garden/index.html

Kids' World: Virgil Life Science Activities
http://www.kidsworld.com/kidsworld/virgil/activity/life/
vwexp001.htm

Seeds of Life
http://versicolores.ca/seedsoflife/index.html

Index/Word List

air, 17
birds, 13
bloom, 5
colors, 7
drop, 13
flower, 5, 7, 9, 11, 13, 21
food, 17
ground, 9, 13
grow, 5, 7, 11, 15, 17, 21
hairs, 15
hole, 9
nature, 11
people, 9

places, 13
plant, 5, 9, 11, 19, 21
root, 21
scatter, 13
seed, 5, 7, 9, 11, 13, 15, 17, 19
shapes, 7
sizes, 7
soil, 9, 11, 17, 21
stem, 21
warmth, 17
water, 9, 17, 19
wind, 15

Word Count: **210**
Early-Intervention Level: **8**

Editorial Credits
Lois Wallentine, editor; James Franklin, design; Michelle L. Norstad, photo research

Photo Credits
Marc Auth, 12
KAC Productions/Kathy Adams Clark, 8, 18
Dwight Kuhn, cover, 16
William Muñoz, 6
Cheryl R. Richter, 4
Root Resources/Ted Farrington, 1
Dan Suzio, 10, 20
Mark Turner, 14

24